40 Days IN HIS PRESENCE

BEVERLY WILLIAMS

40 Days in His Presence
Copyright © 2021 by Beverly Williams

All rights reserved. No part of this publication may be reproduced, distributed, or transmitted in any form or by any means, including photocopying, recording, or other electronic or mechanical methods, without the prior written permission of the author, except in the case of brief quotations embodied in critical reviews and certain other non-commercial uses permitted by copyright law.

ISBN
978-1-956161-76-2 (Paperback)
978-1-956161-75-5 (eBook)

Day 1

Trust in the Lord with all your heart, and lean not on your own understanding; in all your ways acknowledge Him and He shall direct your path.

Proverbs 3:4–5

Rest easy in the knowledge that I am all knowing. I have everything under control. Stop overthinking. Stop over analysing, and turn the matter over to Me. I have the matter in hand. I have this covered, and I have all of the answers. The challenges are not too big for Me. Let go of your anxiety and limited understanding. I am your anchor, and I am the solution to every challenge that assaults your mind at this time. Take your position, and command worry to leave you alone. It is not your companion; it is your enemy. Part company with worry. Insist on its departure immediately! You have My authority to do so. It is your right! Take captive every negative thought that has dominion, and keep your focus sure and steady. I am leading and guiding you every step of the way. I am watching you and strengthening and ordering your every move. You can trust My judgement!

Prayer:

Father, I thank you for the assurance of your complete control over my circumstances, and I am truly sorry for not trusting You on this issue (Philippians 4:6–7). You have not given me a spirit of fear and intimidation, and I acknowledge this to be the case right now (2 Timothy 1:7). I choose to take captive every anxious and nagging thought. I refuse to worry about it any longer (2 Corinthians 10:5). In Jesus's name, amen!

Day 2

*Being confident of this very thing that He who
has begun a good work in you is able to complete
it until the day of Jesus Christ.*

Philippians 1:6

I have not finished with you yet! I am a master craftsman, and with intricate precision, sensitivity, and care, I am fashioning and forming you for My unique and exclusive purpose. I am using you even in the midst of the choices that you have had to make and the choices that were made for you. The situation may have gotten out of hand, but you are very much in the palm of My hand. I am upholding you. My righteous right hand is your shade and cover. I will turn everything around. Your feelings of vulnerability will be used to your advantage. I have not abandoned or forgotten you. I am closer to you than you think. Don't look at their faces or be dismayed by their bravado. Their foolishness will be exposed, and you will be seen in a totally different light. I am building your reputation, which is more important and of more value to Me than the most expensive perfume (Ecclesiastes 7:1). Your reputation goes before you as you yield to My Spirit.

Prayer:

Lord, I thank You that You knitted me together in my mother's womb (Psalm 139:13). You have specific plans and purposes in mind for me (Jeremiah 29:11). I know in my heart of hearts that You will have Your way (Genesis 50:20). Your blueprint for my life was set in place before my birth (Jeremiah 1:5). I thank You that my renewed confidence in You is not in vain and that You don't disappoint those who trust in You (Romans 5:5). Amen!

Day 3

The Lord is a man of war; the Lord is His Name!

Exodus 15:3

Be bold, and do not be afraid. I will fight your battle. Do not say that your strength is insufficient. My strength comes into its own when you need Me most. I know the weakness of your enemies. Your ally is stronger than your enemy. I am your ally! I will make a public spectacle of those who undermine the strength of spirit within you. Look at your giant the way David did. Sing and make melody in your heart in the face of the fierceness of the battle. Even though you do not feel like giving praise, do it anyway. Press in and give Me thanks in the midst of the seeming melee. My spirit that is strong in you shall overcome. The more you praise Me, the stronger your faith will become—and the weaker the enemy in your midst. Give Me the praise that is due. The sacrifice of praise and the fruit of your lips in praise to the one and only true God will be your weapon in this fight (Hebrews 13:15)! Those who know their God shall do great exploits (Daniel 11:32), because greater is He that is in you than he that is within the world (1 John 4:4). I am your ally!

Prayer:

Thank You for the victory, Lord! Thank You that I am on the winning side and that I am destined to win (2 Corinthians 2:14). Thank You that You are making me an overcomer and that the enemy of my soul is defeated (Revelation 12:11). Thank You that you have made me more than a conqueror in You and that I don't have to be defeated (Romans 8:37). I praise You and choose to make Your praise glorious (Psalm 66:2)! In Jesus's mighty name! Amen!

Day 4

*There is gold and a multitude of rubies, but the
lips of knowledge are a precious jewel.*

Proverbs 20:15

Let the words of your mouth and the meditations of your heart be in one accord. Let your words build up and edify your hearers and indeed your own soul! From the treasury of My presence, let the overflow of your heart be a force for blessing and kindness. Be kind and wise with your words about others. Keep watch over your speech. Keep watch over the attitude of your heart. Your tongue cannot bless and curse at the same time (James 3:9). Revere and respect the authority figures in your life with your words. Your words can be a force for good and evil, so let them be words that are seasoned with salt. Let them be not bitter or angry but soothing and kind (Colossians 4:6). The words of the wise are gracious. Do not be drawn into arguments. Have peace with your neighbour. Settle your disputes quickly. Don't allow the dust to settle, and don't give place to the root of bitterness. Speak kindly and turn from being always right. Be wise in your use of words, and your voice will be heard. Be wise in your words, and your counsel will be like honey in the ears of your hearers. Give attention to the use of your words so that your advice will be heeded and your voice will be heard.

Prayer:

Forgive me, Lord, for being less than gracious with speech about others. My words have not always been in keeping with one who is called of God and who seeks to please You. Help me to watch my words and put a guard over my mouth (Proverbs 10:19). Help me to respect those who are authority figures in my life, because they exist for my good (Romans 13:3). Help me to build bridges and mend the walls where relationships have soured (Matthew 5:23–24). With regard to my negative attitude and speech in connection with leadership figures, I take them back right now (Ecclesiastes 10:20). Thank You for hearing my voice on this issue and for helping me to grow in the knowledge that the tongues of the wise use knowledge rightly but the mouths of fools pour forth foolishness (Proverbs 15:2). Amen.

Day 5

Great peace have those who love Your Law and
nothing causes them to stumble.

Psalm 119:165

The Prince of Peace dwells with those who take My word at face value. Mine is the voice of reason. Mine is the voice of calm. I am the voice of stress-free living. I am the voice of rest and freedom from anxiety and deliverance from fear. The King of love is your stress buster. I am the King of love. Allow Me to have greater access to every chamber of your heart and every chamber of your life, and you will find the rest your soul hankers for. Allow My love to enfold you. Let the blanket of My love comfort your heart and release you from the cares and burdens that fill your soul when you try to do life without Me. My word is truth and will teach you My ways. If you will listen, My word is the elixir and remedy to the modern ills that depress the heart and oppress the mind. Be at peace with yourself, and be at peace in your world. Give Me the prime position—the central place in your heart—and you will find genuine rest for your soul. I will be as close to you as you want Me to be.

Prayer:

Thank You, Lord, that I have uninterrupted peace when my heart, my gaze, and my mind are anchored in You (Isaiah 26:3). Your word is my shield, my strength, and an ever-present help in time of trouble (Psalm 46:1). You are always in the midst and always close by. I am not alone. Your loving-kindness towards me is constant. Help me not to forget that You are never far away and that You will never leave me or forsake me (Hebrews 13:5). In Jesus's name!

Day 6

When a man's ways please the Lord, He makes
even his enemies to be at peace with him.

Proverbs 16:7

My ways are not your ways, and neither are My thoughts your thoughts. Humble yourself in My sight; be small in your thinking. Right now it is about looking up and not around you. Look at Me and not at them! This is not about you and your rights; it is about Me. Pleasing Me. Doing that which I desire. All eyes may be upon you, but don't fall for anything that will stop you from allowing Me to fight in your corner. You don't need to lift a finger or say a word. I am your defender. Hide behind Me. It is My battle and not yours. Vengeance belongs to Me. Be patient and hold your peace. Avoid confrontations and altercations. It only causes harm and gives your enemy ammunition. Let the peace of God be the umpire of your heart at this time (Colossians 3:15).

Prayer:

Lord I choose not to fret or to be anxious about what I do not understand about my situation (Psalm 37:8). I know that one with You is a majority, no matter how things may look right now. Help me to control my anger and my frustration. I know that the proud in heart are at loggerheads with Your heart and that is not where I want to be (James 4:6). I ask for Your forgiveness and grace to help me to keep the peace at this time. Help me, oh God, so that I don't sin against You in spite of my anger (Ephesians 4:26). Amen!

Day 7

A merry heart does good like medicine, but a broken spirit dries the bones.

Proverbs 17:22

Laughter is like medicine. Its medicinal qualities will lighten the load and lessen the burden. I laugh at the antics of My enemies (Psalm 2:4). You do likewise. Laugh at your enemies and your detractors. Learn to laugh. Choose to laugh in the face of challenges. It is not denial. It is denying the enemy of your soul from getting the better of you. Make the decision to be the head and not the tail in such circumstances (Deuteronomy 28:13). To laugh and not to moan. The joy of the Lord is your strength (Nehemiah 8:10). Show gratitude without grumbling in the face of your challenges.

Prayer:

Lord, it is difficult to laugh when things are not going so well. It is hard to keep going when things don't go as expected and plans fail to come to fruition, but I choose to praise You in spite of everything (Habakkuk 3:17). I choose to laugh and be joyful in You because You can turn things around. You can turn that which was meant for harm and discouragement into something good (Genesis 50:20). I trust You in this because of Your never-ending love for me (Lamentations 3:22–23). Amen!

Day 8

For we are to God the fragrance of Christ among those who are being saved and among those who are perishing.

2 Corinthians 2:15

Your personal convictions will not always be welcome to those who matter to you. But those who you gently correct or rebuke through your actions (not necessarily your words) will ultimately see you as an invaluable friend. You will be seen as an asset. Be true and be honest with yourself and with those who you are concerned about. Let your presence effuse Jesus in your relationships. As you do, your life will speak for itself. Remember that your actions will sometimes speak louder than your words. Your lifestyle will speak for itself. Your friends may think you strange, but continue in what you have already learned and have become convinced of (2 Timothy 3:14).

Prayer:

Father, thank You for understanding me. Thank You that I am fearfully and wonderfully made (Psalm 139:14). I am Your handiwork for You to use as You see fit to bless others. Thank You that You care about us being honest with one another and that, although it is not easy to watch some of the things that some of my close friends and family are saying and doing, I will stick to what I know is right by You. Help me to resist the temptation to say what they want to hear just to remain friends. I choose not to flatter because I desire true friendship and respect from them for the glory of Your name (Proverbs 28:23). I know that all things will work together for good because Your ultimate aim is to build in me the image and character of Your Son, Jesus (Romans 8:28–29). This is my prayer, in Jesus's name.

Day 9

Arise therefore, go down and go with them, doubting nothing…

Acts 10:20

Trust My guidance; trust My leading. Follow My "dance steps," My timing, My rhythm. Dance to the rhythm of My Spirit. The beat of My drum. Keep the pace. Keep the time. I am orchestrating; I am the maestro for this particular scene in your life. Trust My timing. It is synchronised for you for such a time as this (Esther 4:14). Listen to My timing and tune in to My wavelength. Stick close by, and you will keep in step with the spirit. Do not run ahead of Me, but do not lag behind either. (Galatians 5:25). Timing is everything right now, so don't waver. Be like the wise virgins who were prepared, ready, expectant, and not influenced by the naïveté of popular opinion, fads, or patterns of behaviour. Keep your focus. Keep your pace. Run your race and run it to win. Your prize awaits you! Go with the current of My leading, guidance, and direction.

Prayer:

Heavenly Father, I am used to making my own decisions and following my own hunches assessments and opinions. Nevertheless, Lord, I know that this faith walk is about trusting in You wholeheartedly. With complete abandon, I agree to give You the reins at this time in order to see the results I am looking for. The end results are in Your hands (Proverbs 3:4–6). Thank You, Lord!

Day 10

But without faith it is impossible to please Him, for He who comes to God must believe that He is, and that He is a rewarder of those who diligently seek Him.

Hebrews 11:6

Those who come to Me at their appointed watch, day after day, to listen to My voice shall not leave My presence disappointed or put to shame. My still, small voice is heard by those who give ear to Me. I strengthen you on the inside as you hold to My word and My ways. Keep your heart pure and your hands clean by My spirit. Self-effort has no place in My presence. Openness and transparency before Me will draw Me closer to you and give you wisdom beyond your experience and the expectations of others. So don't try to hide those things, those areas in your heart that need My touch. Open up to Me so that your healing will come. Be vulnerable in My presence. That is when true strength, exultation, and life in the spirit will come. People will marvel at your insight and timely words of encouragement because of the time you spend in My presence. Curl up with Me, and be prepared and empowered to do life with your loving Heavenly Father. Your rewards await you!

Prayer:

Lord, You created me to know You at a deeper level. You created me for relationship, for a regular audience with You, to spend time with You. That is Your delight and Your desire because You are a relational God. You want to share the secrets of Your heart (John 15:15), but I find it difficult to keep diligent and keep my appointments with You. Help me with this, Lord. Help me with my weakness in accordance with Your grace (2 Corinthians 12:9). I want to grow and add to the practical knowledge that comes by sitting at Your feet and hearing and doing Your word as Mary did (Luke 10:39). Help me to have this as my overarching desire so that Your healing touch may bring about a lasting change and untold pleasures! In Jesus's name. Amen.

Day 11

But be doers of the word, and not hearers only, deceiving yourselves.

James 1:22

Truth is more practice than theory. It is about inner transformation more than the accumulation of information. Wisdom is proved right by her actions (Matthew 11:19 NIV). Act on My word and you will prove Me right. Let your actions speak and your words be few. Then you will give an answer to your detractors, the naysayers, and the doubters. Never mind them or their opinions and doubts; you follow Me by walking in obedience. They may not understand you, but I understand those who follow Me. I get it! Shallow ground will not yield rich fruit. Those who bear fruit in their lives are those who give ear to My word and walk out My word with clean hands and a pure heart. Through wisdom, a house is built and by understanding it is established (Proverbs 24:3). True know edge is wisdom applied in an appropriate and timely manner. He who observes you secretly will see that your integrity is rewarded openly. Maintain your integrity in the place of My presence, and you will not be disappointed. Be patient!

Prayer:

Lord, please keep me from self-deception. Please deliver me from being smug about the knowledge I have of Your word and from being overly concerned about what others think of me. Forgive me for my apathy in applying Your word from my heart (James 4:17). I want to taste and experience the goodness that comes from the practical obedience to Your word because I understand that doing Your word brings blessing (Psalm 34:8). It is knowing and doing Your word that brings light, revelation, confidence, security, and direction (Psalm 119:130). Help me, Lord, as I navigate this season in my life. Amen!

Day 12

Do not be deceived: Evil company corrupts good habits.

1 Corinthians 15:33

Your friendships determine your moral compass. Your associates will determine who you are and your destiny in this season. The company of fools will find they will come to ruin (Proverbs 13:20). Do not be unequally yoked (2 Corinthians 6:14). Do not enter into agreements without consulting with Me or seeking the counsel of the wise and learned in your midst. Wrong associations will lead you into bondage. Be selective with those you confide in. Extricate yourself quickly from unwholesome unions. Do not overcommit yourself. Wise counsel is your safety net and will keep you from wasting time and emotional energy on relationships that are draining and unrewarding.

Prayer:

Loving Father, You are so wise and all-knowing. You know my coming out and my going in because Your desire is to protect and preserve me from all harm (Psalm 121:8). You know that those who keep company with wise men will become wise (Proverbs 13:20). Help me to choose my friends with discretion and discernment. Help me to associate with all those who love You, who choose to relate to You, and who are sympathetic to the values that espouse Your cause with all integrity (Psalm 119:63). You know the plans You have in mind for me and the role that the right relationships have to play in those plans. I want to choose my friends carefully. Keep me from going astray (Proverbs 12:26). Amen!

Day 13

Do you see a man who excels in his work?
He will stand before kings; He will not serve
before unknown men.

Proverbs 22:29

The diligent man is trustworthy and destined for leadership. You will emerge as a leader before your peers and contemporaries if you are single-minded. Work quietly, efficiently, and effectively. Like the ant and the locust, the diligent man maintains a strong work ethic (Proverbs 6:6–8; Proverbs 30:27). The diligent man does not work with man alone in view. Be diligent and faithful and work to give pleasure and honour to your maker. Your ultimate focus is heavenwards and motivation is twofold: the present and the future. Be mindful of Me, your Creator in this season. There is a season for everything. Promotion and recognition will come. They will come when you least expect it, but it will come. I sit in the highest heavens and see everything and will move things around on your behalf. I will blow your trumpet! Others will praise you and acknowledge your work at the highest level. Exaltation will come! Your name will be on the lips of those in high office because of your excellence and reliability on delivery.

Prayer:

Thank You for the value You place on diligence, Lord. I understand that laziness is abhorrent to You, so please take away that tendency from me (Proverbs 12:24). Teach me to be diligent in all that my hands find to do. Help me to do whatever You give me to do with zeal, passion, and responsibility, knowing that You see all things (Ecclesiastes 9:10). Thank You too for the gifts You have given to me. Help me to excel in whatever gifts I have received from You so that my growth and progress give honour to You. I know that the gifts are powerless and meaningless if I don't show love to others so help me to grow in this area of my character in word and in deed (2 Corinthians 8:7). In Jesus's name, amen!

Day 14

*And it shall be, when you hear the sound of
marching in the tops of the mulberry trees,
then you shall advance quickly. For then the Lord
shall go out before you to strike the
camp of the Philistines.*

2 Samuel 5:24

My ways and methods of executing My plans are unique. My battle plan has been established and is unique for this situation. You may feel like you are ill-equipped, but you are fit for My purpose. You are My choice, My chosen instrument for this season, and you are in good company. To some, your appointment defies human logic, but spiritual things are spiritually discerned and My weaponry will always confound the wisdom of the philosophers, pundits, and those who think they know better than Me. To the devious, I will show myself shrewd (Proverbs 18:26), and those who are wily in their own eyes shall be taken by surprise. Their demise shall be swift and sudden. You who wait for Me shall not be ashamed or embarrassed (Psalm 25:3). He who is within you is greater than He that is in the world! I will use you to confound My accusers. Those who honour Me, I will honour (1 Samuel 2:30).

Prayer:

Dear Father, I am lost for words! You are showing me that Your ways are not my ways and neither are Your thoughts anything like the way I think. (Isaiah 55:8). You are a master strategist who is just and perfect in all of Your ways. You are a rock! My rock! Your ways are beyond my understanding! Thank You, Lord, for the assurance of Your presence and victory. Thank You that You work behind the scenes and knit everything together for good to bring me to the place where I am formed into the image of Christ (Romans 8:28–29). You are an amazing God! Thank You, Jesus!

Day 15

And the God who answers by fire, He is God!

1 Kings 18:24

I am the God who answers by fire! I shall mount an offensive against your detractors. My response shall be decisive and unmistakable. Your arms are strong for the task, and you shall be seen and known as the one who has God's ear. So keep trusting. Keep listening. I am watching. I am not asleep. I am orchestrating behind the scenes for your good and not your harm, although that may not appear to be the case on the surface. I will undo what has been done in secret. Greater and more numerous are those with you than you think (2 Kings 6:16). I will open the eyes of your understanding. I am your God.

Prayer:

Thank You for Your presence with me and that You are on my side! Thank You that You are for me and not against me (Romans 8:31). One with You is a majority, which means that You are unshakeable, immovable, and utterly trustworthy. You are not to be underestimated, and I am eternally grateful to You. Amen!

Day 16

The lazy man does not roast what he
took in hunting but diligence is a man's
precious possession.

Proverbs 12:27

Finish the job. Finish what you have started; you are still in the race. You have time. Do not be half-hearted with the work I have given you to do. The finish line is in reach. It is within your grasp. Apply yourself to the job in hand, and stimulate the passion and drive that will carry you through to completion. The opportunity is at hand. Utilise it. Do not lose momentum or lose the vision that I have given you for this task. Greater opportunities await your gifting and abilities at the completion of this task. This is only the beginning. For since the beginning of the world, men have neither heard nor perceived by the ear, nor has the eye seen … a God like Me who works behind the scenes on your behalf. You have a lot going for you. (Isaiah 64:4). Redouble your efforts, and stay on track.

Prayer:

Lord, forgive me for my half-heartedness and apathy. I am struggling to find the momentum and the motivation to go on right now. I know You are cheering me on and encouraging me to complete the course (Hebrews 12:1). Help me to keep my focus and separate myself from those distractions—legitimate or otherwise— right now. I know I am dragging my feet and things are taking longer than they ought. Fill me anew with fresh grace, faith, and life in You, I pray. In Jesus's name, amen!

Day 17

> Let your light so shine before men,
> that they may see your good works
> and glorify your Father in heaven.
>
> Matthew 5:16

Your light will shine for all to see when you walk in alignment with My will for you in this season. This is a critical time for you. My radiance and presence in your life will be clearly on display if you trust Me. Your radiance and reputation will go before you when you consistently make the right choices behind the scenes. What it looks like to others doesn't matter. What it looks like to Me does. What you do in secret will be seen in the open spaces. Do those things that please Me, even when no one is looking and even though it may be painful. It is not about what others think of you. It is what I say about you that carries weight and makes the difference. As you are mindful of Me, your reputation before others will grow and be established for your good. A good reputation is better than expensive perfume (Ecclesiastes 7:1 GNT). A good reputation is priceless. Trust the process!

Prayer:

Father God, Your wisdom is faultless and Your counsel is for my best interest. I know You are all-knowing and You make every crooked path straight (Isaiah 45:2). Go before me so that I can break through to the place where Your light will shine through me for the glory and honour of Your holy name. Amen.

Day 18

Surely goodness and mercy shall follow me
all the days of my life; and I will dwell in the
house of the Lord forever.

Psalm 23:6

My goodness, My mercy, and My grace towards you are limitless. I surround you with love and kindness and rejoice over you with songs of joy (Zephaniah 3:17). Your life is a witness. The multifaceted goodness of My grace shines through you in more ways than one. Your life—witness and testimony—is shedding My life and light through your good deeds and acts of service towards others. Such acts of kindness attract My attention because of your selfless investment in others. You are sowing into the lives of others, and I will have others invest in you. Every time you do go d to others, you are pleasing Me. You are serving Me. You are honouring Me. I am being exalted. My grace and mercy towards you will be a constant in your life as you continue to keep such an attitude close to your heart. I will be mindful of you and will not forget your labour of love for Me and the love you show towards others who love Me (Hebrews 6:10).

Prayer:

Thank You, Lord, for the refreshing encouragement from Your word today. You send rain on the earth and send waters in the field (Job 5:10), and so You have done on my life today. You are full of goodness and have caused me to flourish. Your favour is more than I truly deserve, but I am grateful for the continuous outpouring of love and faithfulness that You show me. I have found favour in Your sight, and it is because of Your grace and kindness towards me. Thank You, Jesus!

Day 19

Go and sin no more.

John 8:11

There is no condemnation. Guilt does not belong to you. Your accusers are shortsighted. The "accuser of the brethren" has had the rug taken from under his feet, and so have your accusers. Your mistakes shall not be counted against you. Having owned up to your past mistakes, you have been forgiven. Go and do likewise. Forgive those who have sinned against you. Settle your disputes quickly. Own up to your faults and shortcomings in all humility, and you will see vindication. Exercise wisdom, do the right thing, walk in forgiveness, and you will be vindicated.

Prayer:

There is none wiser and more loving than You, Heavenly Father. Thank You for Your unwearying love and endless mercy towards me (Lamentations 3:22–23). It is far more than I deserve. You are generous in Your kindness to me, in spite of my faults and wrongdoing, time and time again. Your patience is a constant source of strength and encouragement through it all. I am comforted by Your assurance of forgiveness: it fills me with hope again. For a righteous man may fall seven times and rise again, but the wicked shall fall by calamity (Proverbs 24:16). You are my deliverer, my hope, and my God. Thank You, Lord! Amen!

Day 20

You are of God, little children, and have overcome
them because He that is in you is greater
than he that is in the world.

1 John 4:4

He has nothing on you. He cannot defeat you. Put on your armour and shield your mind; take your position. You are on the winning side! If God is for you, who can be against you (Romans 8:31)? Victory is yours! Hold your peace and allow My presence to give you the strength and true perspective of the situation. Keep your gaze strong and firmly fixed on Me. You are not alone: I am within and without. Do not rely on your own strength but on My ability and grace. The pressure to give in may seem great, but My grace is sufficient for your current situation. Be strong and don't let go.

Prayer:

Lord, You are undeniably able to do much more than I could ask, think, or imagine (Ephesians 3:20). You are off the scale in your immeasurable power and authority! It is not by my might or my will; it is all about You. Nothing can happen outside of Your permission, and I can see that You are teaching me and training me to stand in faith at this time. You are truly training my hands for war and my fingers for battle, and I take refuge in You (Psalm 144:1–2). Amen!

Day 21

Great men are not always wise, neither do the
aged always understand justice.

Job 32:9

The wisdom of the great and the learned among you is not always sound, sensible, or entirely appropriate. Age and experience do not always guarantee sound counsel. The book of Proverbs tells you that the fear of the Lord brings wisdom and understanding. The psalmist said that he had more understanding than his teachers (Psalm 119:99). There are times when it is right not to defer out of respect. It is possible for the least among you to have more godly insight at times than those who have accrued knowledge and experience over time and life experience. Such people have learnt to sit at My feet and have been Taught of Me to not "lean on your own understanding" is good and wise counsel, but don't be entirely dependent on the understanding of others either. Balance, weigh, and measure with the wisdom that I give to those who ask. If you lack wisdom, come to Me. I am the fount of all knowledge, and you can trust My guidance. I will not let you down.

Prayer:

Father, You are not short of knowledge or understanding. You tell me to knock, seek, and ask. (Matthew 7:7), and You have all the right answers and wisdom aplenty. Yet somehow it seems easier and takes much less effort to ask someone to pray for me or to get the opinion of another. Help me to not always take things at face value, no matter how well meaning. Help me to test and discern and take responsibility for the counsel I receive. You store up sound wisdom for the upright. You are a shield to those who walk uprightly (Proverbs 2:7). Thank You for the treasure trove of wisdom that is there for the taking. Amen!

Day 22

I say to you there is no one who has left house or brothers or sisters or father or mother or wife or children or lands for My sake and the gospel's who shall not receive a hundredfold now in this time— houses and brothers and sisters and mothers and children and lands, with persecutions— and in the age to come eternal life.

Mark 10:29–30

The things that I have in store for you will not always be handed to you on a plate. Kingdom values calls for a kingdom mind-set. A kingdom mind-set calls for kingdom living, and kingdom living calls for a heart that is set apart and loves and trusts Me throughout the seasons of life's ups and downs. Jesus paid with His life, and at times you will be called to pay a high price in order to walk the seeming tightrope of obedience. Yet rest and be relieved of all anxiety. I am your God and I have good gifts and blessings in store for you. I will show myself strong on your behalf. Such gifts, blessings, and opportunities are laid up for you to possess. They have your name on them and will come about through your walk of obedience, faith, perseverance, and trust. As you learn to trust Me on your journey, life takes on new meaning, and so do life's challenges. My perspective is different from yours, but My rewards and My victories are much sweeter when I am in the driving seat.

Prayer:

Dear Lord, You are the God of the breakthrough (2 Samuel 5:20). Where I am feeling resistance, I know that You will come through and that I must stand in the knowledge of the fact that You are a conqueror, my rock, and a very present help in time of trouble (Psalm 46:1). I bless Your holy name for Your oversight and protection on my life because You are ordering my steps (Psalm 37:23). Amen!

Day 23

The race is not to the swift nor the battle to the strong, nor bread to the wise, nor riches to men of understanding, nor favour to men of skills; but time and chance happen to them all.

Ecclesiastes 9:11

Enjoy the season of opportunity that you have before you. You have not arrived in this position by accident. Make the best of it. It is an unusual route to bigger and better things for you. You would not naturally be in the running, but you will find yourself in places and positions of privilege that I have been orchestrating because I work in extraordinary ways. My timing is perfect. Make the most of the time you have been given; it is a season in which you will reap a return on your investment. An unexpected harvest awaits you!

Prayer:

Thank You, Lord, that You make a road in the wilderness and rivers in the desert (Isaiah 43:19). You open doors that no man can shut (Revelation 3:8). No one can take the credit for what You alone can do. You are amazing God. Help me to do my very best at this time and season. You are so faithful. Thank You for what You are about to achieve through me. In Jesus's name. Amen.

Day 24

*A word fitly spoken is like apples of gold
in settings of silver.*

Proverbs 25:11

The finest counsellor on the face of this earth is Me. Drink of Me. Learn of Me. Work with Me. My yoke is easy. There is nothing perverse or crooked about My ways. They are plain to him who sincerely tries to understand with a mind and heart for truth. I have the solution to every problem, and those who possess such wisdom and live their lives in the light of such wisdom shall never be disappointed. They shall be elevated. Your experiences have given you exposure to the power and source of such wisdom: My Spirit. Do not be afraid to share the wisdom and knowledge that you have uncovered at this time. Give Him the glory. It would be prudent to do so!

Prayer:

Thank You, Lord, that You are teaching me to make wisdom my sister and understanding my next of kin (Proverbs 7:4). The two are not inseparable, and life without these gifts would be impossible. I know that these abilities come from You. I ask that You would please continue to give me the wisdom I need for myself and for others. In Your precious name, I pray. Amen!

Day 25

The joy of the Lord is your strength.

Nehemiah 8:10

My joy is a gift to you. It is your buffer against sorrows and the storms of life's trials. It cannot be manufactured and operates outside of your emotions. It operates objectively and not subjectively. It centres around a place of diligent trust in My word in spite of the circumstances. It revolves around Me as your focus in the midst of everything. When you walk according to My word, peace and joy are by-products. So if you don't have My joy or peace, ask yourself some tough questions. Do some soul-searching in the light of My word, your relationship with Me, and your relationship with others. We cannot say that we love God if we are at loggerheads with others. As far as it depends on you, live peaceably with others forgo your rights and honour Me in your relationships. If you fail to honour Christ in your witness and relationships, you lose out and your joy diminishes over time, so keep your calling and election sure. Keep going deeper and your joy in the Lord strong.

Prayer:

Dear Lord, You are the essence and the strength of life and I need You in my life more and more. My relationships with others and with You need a review, and I know I have some work to do. Though weeping may endure for a night, joy comes in the morning (Psalm 30:5). This shortfall in true lasting peace has gone on for a long time. I am not perfect, and I am looking to You to please help me to mend bridges in all humility, mercy, and purity, for this is the fruit of righteousness and it is the pathway to true peace and joy (James 3:17– 18). Please forgive me for holding out on You and the relevant friends and family members for so long. In Jesus's name, I pray. Amen!

Day 26

I am ready to perform My word.

Jeremiah 1:12

I deliver on My word. My promises are cast iron. I do not speak vain or empty words. My words are intentional and carry weight and authority. When I say I will do it, I will. What I say will be done, shall be done. I am the caretaker of My word. I will not allow My word to fall to the ground unfulfilled, no matter how long it takes for that word to come into its season: it will bear fruit. It will yield fruit. My word is fruit bearing and it will yield for the glory and honour of My name! The passage of time is not the issue. Passing the test of hearing the word and mixing it with faith is the crux of the matter, because it is the condition of the heart that can influence the final outcome for certain prophetic declarations. Make sure you meet the conditions where appropriate by abiding in Me. You will not be disappointed. I have declared My purpose before the appointed time to demonstrate the power of My Word.

Prayer:

Heavenly Father, You are the vine, and I choose to cling to You as a branch would a tree in order to bear fruit. Help me, Lord, to abide in You so that I can taste of Your goodness and see the truth of Your word bearing fruit in my life. Thank You that Your word is truth. It is rock solid, reliable, and durable and will sustain me in the fiercest storms. I understand that by standing on Your word I can produce a crop that can yield thirtyfold, sixtyfold, or one hundredfold in my life to the glory of Your name (Matthew 13:8). Your word is the bedrock for my faith, and I choose to feed on the faithfulness of Your word to the glory of God, my Father. Amen!

Day 27

A man who isolates himself seeks his own desire;
He rages against all wise judgement.

Proverbs 18:1

Guard against withdrawing and retreating because of anger, disappointment, or humiliation. Be gracious, and learn from the tough experiences. I will vouch for you, if you will trust Me. I will vindicate you and fight on your behalf. Resist the temptation to walk out or run away. Face the music. Stay put. Stay calm. Do not allow your emotions to get the better of you. Build bridges, not barriers. Be angry, but do not sin. Do not become unreachable or unteachable in your anger and disappointment. It will not help your cause or win the battle. To hold on to offence would b a mistake and will distort the good image and reputation that you have. Keep the dialogue open; do not be wise in your own eyes. You forfeit the benefits of having good counsellors around you when you keep your own counsel under such circumstances.

Prayer:

Father, I feel hurt and misunderstood. I don't feel that I have been heard or given a real opportunity to get my point of view across. Help me not to take things into my own hands out of frustration or rejection. Help me to heed good counsel and not to think that my way is the only way as much as I believe this to be the case (Proverbs 12:15). Please be my advisor and advocate on this one. Stand up for my cause and win justice for me, I pray.

Day 28

The wicked flee when no one pursues but the righteous are bold as a lion.

Proverbs 28:1

My authority is not to be sniffed at. It is an authority that guarantees against your defeat. Those who contend with you will have Me to deal with since you are a child of Mine and the apple of My eye. You don't have to fight this battle; just keep praising Me. Keep worshipping Me. I am the King of the ages, the only wise God who will make it apparent to those who are wise in their own eyes that I oppose the proud but give grace to the humble (James 4:6). They shall see their plots and schemes unravel before their eyes. So long as you wait upon Me with clean hands, your hands shall grow stronger and stronger (Job 17:9). Do not be intimidated.

Prayer:

My Father and my God You are the altogether lovely One. There is no flaw in You or in any of Your ways. You know how to manage every problem. You are an amazing God! You are the strength of my life, and You have reminded me that I have nothing to be afraid of. The spirit of fear does not come from You, but love, power, and a sound mind are what You give to me and all those who fear Your name (2 Timothy 1:7). Lord, You see how the proud have risen against me and a mob of violent men have sought my life and have not set You before them (Psalm 86:14). Take my hand and help me to stand firm in You. In Jesus's name!

Day 29

To do evil is like sport to a fool, but a man of understanding has wisdom.

Proverbs 10:23

Avoid entering conversations that compromise your walk and witness. Maintain standards and patterns of behaviour in your speech and conduct that uphold My light. Walk wisely and watch your speech, especially with your interactions with those who don't know Me. Watch your choice of words, tame your tongue. We cannot be blessing and praising God on the one hand and pit one against the other behind closed doors for fun. It is unkind and potentially harmful to you and your hearers. It is costly to your development and maturity. You can stumble your hearers through foolish or coarse and unhelpful contentions, and even what may appear to be harmless joking can harm your reputation and standing if you are careless with your words. A little leaven leavens the whole lump (Galatians 5:9).

Prayer:

Lord, You are the master of communication. Help me to exercise self-control over the words of my mouth and the meditations of my heart (Psalm 19:14). Sin is never far away where conversation is flowing. Please give me the wisdom and sensitivity I need to exercise self-restraint with my frivolous speech and conduct in trying situations, for Your name's sake. Amen.

Day 30

Not by might nor by power but by my Spirit, says the Lord of hosts.

Zechariah 4:7

I am the one who builds, plants, establishes, and lays foundations. You cannot build apart from Me. Good ideas are only good ideas when I am directing, leading, or advising. Without Me it is vain; it is futile to embark on any project that is not of My Spirit. The letter kills, but the life of the Spirit brings increase, strength, favour provision, momentum, and vision. My vision will not bring confusion. Self-effort is powerless, but with Me all things are possible. Build with My strategy, and you will avoid wasting time and energy on presumption and false starts. Remember King David had the heart and vision to build a temple for Me, but I had not chosen Him to oversee the work (1 Kings 8:19). Sometimes the vision has to flow with a particular season. Collaborate with Me. Get to know My timings and My seasons and you will see the difference when you work with My Spirit (Galatians 5:16).

Prayer:

Lord, You encourage us to ask, seek, and knock (Matthew 7:7). I am asking for more of You. I am asking for more of Your enabling, Your equipping, and Your insight—like the men of Issachar who were politically sound and astute with Your seasons and timings (1 Chronicles 12:32). Teach me Your way, O Lord. I will walk in Your truth. I want to avoid the pitfalls and the pain that so often come with presumption and lack of knowledge (Hosea 4:6). In Jesus's name. Amen.

Day 31

And do not be drunk with wine in which is dissipation; but be filled with the Holy Spirit.

Ephesians 5:18

Open your heart to Me. Drink of My Spirit I will quench your thirst. Hunger for Me, and I will fill you up. I am your Father. I see your inner longings and yearnings. I alone can satisfy. I alone can satiate. I alone can bring healing to your inner most being. As you trust and yield, you will discover new depths and heights in Me. As you let go, you will soar and you will discover things about Me and about you that will make for your good and not for your harm. You will discover My plans go way beyond your wildest dreams and imaginations. Increase your appetite for Me. Seek Me. Stir yourself up to seek Me. Let Me demonstrate My love. Sow to the Spirit and crucify the flesh with all its passion so that the life of My Spirit will fill, heal, and deliver you! Enjoy your freedom! Enjoy the new you!

Prayer:

Lord, You bid me to come. I hear You, Father. I hear You inviting me into Your presence. Your calm and soothing words of affirmation are too hard to resist. I hear You asking me to come away with You (Song of Solomon 2:10). I am learning that my faith and trust in You determine the course of my journey. No one else can make the journey on my behalf. My relationship with You is not dependent on what others think or say of me. It is about taking time to listen to You and allowing You access to my heart and life on a daily basis. I open my heart wider still because I know You love me and I can always trust You. In Jesus's name, amen!

Day 32

For we are His workmanship created in Christ Jesus for good works which God prepared beforehand that we should walk in them.

Ephesians 2:10

You are fearfully and wonderfully made (Psalm 139:14). You are known about and knitted together for a unique plan—a unique purpose. You were known by Me before your parents knew you. You are not a replica of someone else and your gifts and particular talents are unique to you. Do not compare yourself with another. Do not compare your achievements with another. The plan is for you to fulfil your purpose for you this side of heaven. Follow My blueprint. Follow My master plan. There is favour upon your life to achieve and fulfil your purpose. You are destined to win. Destined to overcome. Destined to conquer those fears and those doubts. The Lord has a good work for you and is doing a good work in you. He has elected you for this day and generation. You are not an afterthought in God. Do not underestimate the role you have to play and the gifts that will accentuate that role. You are fit for purpose!

Prayer:

Thank You, Lord, for my life's purpose. It is good to know that You know the plans You have for me (Jeremiah 29:11). My life is in Your hands. My days are written in Your book (Psalm 139:16). Please help me to live my life in such a way that it counts. I want every day that I live to count for You and Your purpose for my life. In Jesus's name. Amen.

Day 33

*Now faith is the substance of things hoped for,
the evidence of things not seen.*

Hebrews 11:1

Faith as small as a mustard seed is more than sufficient for Me to work with. Exercise your faith. Let the gift of faith of arise within you. It is not always wisdom to play it safe. Sometimes faith will take risks humanly speaking. Without faith, it is impossible to please God (Hebrews 11:6). To work with Me requires that you are not hemmed in by your own understanding. When the Roman centurion encountered Jesus, He was in no doubt about what Jesus could do for him and the situation he presented Him with. He had not seen the physical manifestation of his request, yet he believed (Matthew 8:5–13). Calling things that are not as yet as though they are is an act of faith. Speaking and living from the language of faith is always appropriate when I have already communicated My intentions (Romans 4:17), so don't back down or back away from what I have already told you and asked you to do.

Prayer:

Lord, You are faithful and with You all things are possible (Matthew 19:26). You are not restricted by the natural because You act outside of this realm. Thank You for the freedom. Thank You for the liberty that faith breeds and enabling grace that comes with it. I thank You for the heroes of faith in the book of Hebrews who have blazed a trail and given me a pattern to work with. In Jesus's name! Amen!

Day 34

So shall My word be that goes forth from My mouth; it shall not return to Me void, But it shall accomplish what I please, And it shall prosper in the thing for which I sent it.

Isaiah 55:11

My word shall not return void when I speak. I will accomplish. I will perform. I will fulfil. I will bring My word to pass for you and your family in this season. My season for you is not passed. It is not over. My grace for this season is not complete. It has not passed. It is not too late. This season is still in its infancy, still in the stage of early flowering. You shall eat and enjoy the fruit of this season with joy and thanksgiving if you will persevere and take advantage and stock of this season. Do not be faint-hearted or double-minded. Take hold of this season with both hands and your whole heart. Keep moving forward. I am with you. My Word is never spoken in vain. It is by My word that this world was created, and it is by My word that your world will see shifts, tremors, and lasting changes in this season. My word is at work and is working in all integrity.

Prayer:

Lord, Your word is truth! It is the very anchor that my soul needs in this trying season. I know that there are times when I need to remind myself that You are very much in control and that Your word has the final say. Everything You do and say is for my benefit, but I admit it doesn't always feel like it.

I ask that You would help me in my unbelief. I know that Your word says that all things are possible to him who believes (Mark 9:23–25). I choose to believe. Amen!

Day 35

A bruised reed he will not break, and a smouldering wick He will not snuff out.

Isaiah 42:3

A bruised wick I will not put out. My sensitivity towards you at this stage is second to none. I see the delicacy of your situation. I see the deep places of your heart. I see the secrets and quiet place of your unspoken yearnings and inner pain and turmoil. I see the fragility of the situation. I am for you and not against you Let Me in. Let Me heal. Let Me do for you what you have need of Me to do. To love on you. To mend and restore that place that has been broken down, to repair the places broken by those who you had trusted. Do not let go of My love for you. I have not changed. My disposition and heart for you is unchanged. Let Me nourish your soul.

Prayer:

Father, Your name has healing properties for those with a heavy heart. Your name is ointment poured forth (Songs of Solomon 1:3). Your empathy and understanding are comforts to me. You have seen my secret tears when my heart is overwhelmed. My tears are stored up in a bottle and You have made a note of each one (Psalm 56:8). You see my pain and the insecurities that I am battling with, and I hand that which is heavy in my heart over to You. Please help me to guard my heart (Proverbs 4:23) as I mend, heal, and overcome the disappointments. In Jesus's name, amen.

Day 36

Bring the whole tithe into the storehouse,
that there may be food in My house,
And try Me now I this, says the Lord of hosts.
If I will not open for you the windows of heaven
and pour out for you such a blessing that there
will not be room enough to receive it.

Malachi 3:10

Do not be tempted to short-change Me in any way. I do not do things by half measures. I am not half-hearted towards you. I am not lukewarm towards you. My heart is fully committed to your growth and expansion in every sense of the word. So why do you doubt My ability to provide for you? To look out for you? To look after you? I will not allow you to b in lack when you honour Me with your resources. I am truly the source of your income. I give you the ability to get wealth in every dimension (Deuteronomy 8:18), so do not doubt My ability to enhance and increase what I have given to you for your care and practical needs. I have all you will ever need at My disposal. Your money I do not need, but what I want most of all is your heart of love for Me. For where your treasure is, there your heart will be also (Matthew 6:21).

Prayer:

Lord, forgive me for holding out on You with my finances. You are my provider and my deliverer, and You own all things. Help me to be a good steward of what You give me. It is not good to withhold unduly. Help me to overcome the resistance to sowing with My finances. Deliver me, I pray!

Day 37

I traverse the way of righteousness,
in the midst of the paths of justice,
that I may cause those who love me to inherit
wealth, that I may fill their treasuries.

Proverbs 8:20–21

I am all-seeing and all-knowing. I miss nothing; My eyes go back and forth throughout the earth (2 Chronicles 16:9) in search of those who serve out of a sincere heart. I reward those whose heart is with Me in all sincerity. This is what I require and look for. This is what I desire. When I see this, I will not withhold My blessing, I cannot withhold My blessing. It is My heart to bless, to reward and to encourage in every sense of the word. I desire that you should thrive and flourish as you hold fast to the word of life.

Prayer:

Lord, You know the way that I take (Job 23:10). I cannot escape Your gaze. Wherever I go, You are there. There is no hiding place from You. Indeed, You are my hiding place (Psalm 32:7). You see my coming in and my going out (Psalm 121:8), and You weigh and test my every action. I am in a privileged position because of Your watchful eye. You see what is done in public and in private, and I know You are a fair and just God who will reward according to what You see. You are a God of equity and justice—there is no favouritism with You.

Day 38

He who walks with integrity walks securely, But
he who perverts his ways will become known.

Proverbs 10:9

Be notorious for the right reasons. Be known for doing the right things for the right reasons. It is not about doing things to impress each other. It is about doing things to please Me. That which is seen by Me and done for Me will be honoured by Me because I see the motives of men's hearts. If you are doing things to please one another or to gain favour from one another, you are setting yourself up for humiliation and disappointment. Do the right thing with the right motive, and that which is done in secret with Me as your audience will be openly acknowledged. Do not let your left hand know what your right hand is doing (Matthew 6:3–4).

Prayer:

Father God, help me to be true to my word and the things that I commit to. I choose to swallow my pride in order to straighten out my motives. You mean for me to live a life that exalts Your ways, and I give up trying to impress for my own gain and taking shortcuts and quick fixes to hide or cover up my shortcomings and weaknesses. You desire truth in the inward parts (Psalm 51:6). Help me to be truly sorry for my behaviour. Obedience to You is better than sacrificing in order to look good and play the part in front of others (1 Samuel 15:22). I am truly sorry. Please help me to change. Amen.

Day 39

The blessings of the Lord make one rich,
and He adds no sorrow with it.

Proverbs 10:22

It is My heart's desire to bless without measure, to give unreservedly, and to give freely and unconditionally. It is in My nature to give in order to bless, to encourage, and to affirm My love for you. Be it spiritual gifts, material things, or acts of kindness, giving in any form is My language of love. I have no ulterior motive other than to bless you and demonstrate My character and nature so that you in turn will want to bless those around you. Receive whatever you are given with grace and gratitude. Know that the gift, whether it is great or small, is ultimately a blessing from Me, your Heavenly Father. There is no price tag or "catch" to My love or caveat to My blessings. Be blessed!

Prayer:

Lord, thank You for Your tender love. Thank You for showing me how to love and bless others with sincerity. Thank You for Your patience with me in my doubt and uncertainty about You and others. Help me to be more gracious and humble in my attitude towards those who are genuine in their desire to be a blessing to me in Jesus's name, amen!

Day 40

> Therefore as we have opportunity,
> let us do good to all men, and especially to those
> who are of the household of faith.
>
> Galatians 6:10

Let your love for people be demonstrated by acts of service. If you love Me, serve others with all sincerity. As you serve others, you are ultimately ministering to My heart and My heart is for people. People matter to Me. As you refresh others, you yourself will be refreshed (Proverbs 11:25). A kind word, a kind gesture, a home visit, bearing with the burden of another: these are all ways in which you will develop a sensitivity to My heart and enrich your soul. Add to your faith in these ways and you will increase your effectiveness in your productivity for My kingdom. Look for ways to demonstrate My relentless love and compassion with all your heart, and you will be blessed.

Prayer:

Thank You, Lord, for Your timely insights and reminders that You are interested in me and my ongoing development and growth; Your acts of kindness and love towards others testify to my discipleship in You (John 13:35). You also remind me that faith without works is dead (James 2:14–16). Help me, Lord, to demonstrate Your heart in loving and sensitive ways so that I can be a credible witness for Your glory. Amen.

About the Author

Beverly Williams is an outstanding Christian woman, servant, and minister, and her writing is born out of her deep devotion to God and years of serving him and his people. Her years of experience and wisdom are now available to us in this inspiring devotional, 40 Days in His Presence. It is her first book.

www.ingramcontent.com/pod-product-compliance
Lightning Source LLC
Chambersburg PA
CBHW021430070526
44577CB00001B/147